AnglePlay®
the Easy Way

by Andi Stanfield and Mary McElvain

Copyright 2017
ISBN-13: 978-1976489570
ISBN-10: 1976489571

Dedication

Thanks to Kevin, Bentley and Kendra who
support our quilting and book publishing dreams.

Special thanks to
Jenna Straface, photographer
and Matthew Elizondo, graphic designer.

AnglePlay® the Easy Way
by Andi Stanfield and Mary McElvain

Table of Contents

Introduction ... 6

Using templates and Choosing Fabric for AnglePlay® designs

1. Blossom Placemats	2. Thistles Table Runner	3. Joyful Noise table runner
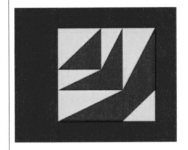		
Templates A, E Pg 11	Templates A, B, G Pg 17	Templates A, B, H Pg 24
4. Fruit Salad	5. Two by Two	6. Birds Flying High
	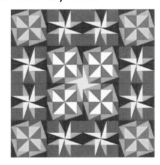	
Template A Pg 31	Templates A, B Pg 37	Templates B, K Pg 45

7. Race Is On	8. Around the Pond	9. Ripples
Templates A, B, H Pg 54	Templates A, G Pg 62	Templates A, B, E, H, I, K Pg 70
10. Tickle My Fancy	11. Echo	12. Spring Training
Templates A, B, H Pg 80	Templates A, B, D, H Pg 87	Templates A, B, H, K Pg 96

Free Motion Quilting Ideas

... 107

Introduction

Margaret J. Miller designed over 200 AnglePlay® blocks in the 1990's. We are greatly indebted to her vision and contribution to the quilting community. She gave us an enormous choice of elements. However, the multitude of choices can be overwhelming to quilters. We are building on Margaret's legacy to reach more quilters. Our goals for this book are:

- To inspire a love of working with AnglePlay® templates to create rich-looking quilts.
- To offer patterns that are beginner-friendly.
- To provide another set of patterns for people already familiar with AnglePlay®.

Two principles guided us in designing the AnglePlay® quilts in this book. We simplified the designs by one, using fewer colors (fabrics) than previously and two, combining AnglePlay® blocks with traditional blocks for our quilts. We also show two versions of each project in order to stimulate ideas for readers and to encourage them to step out of personal comfort zones in terms of color.

None of the quilts in this book require large amounts of any one fabric. That means that you can go to your stash and have fun with a project! (Not that we are negating the fun of shopping...) None of the projects are what we call "labor intensive." That means you can finish a project without a major time investment.

We want to thank our pattern testers. They did a tremendous job in clarifying directions and providing alternate layouts and colorways. They are: Barbara Harrell, Shari Graves, Ann Beam, Helene Block and Michelle Kessler.

As in all of our teaching and writing, we wish quilters three things: to ENJOY, EXPERIMENT and EXCEL!!

General Directions

AnglePlay® quilts are the brainchild of Margaret J. Miller. She introduced them to the world with <u>AnglePlay® Blocks (2005)</u> and <u>Stunning AnglePlay® Quilts (2008)</u>. Margaret designed blocks using elongated triangles and pieced triangles with a set of templates to create masterful quilts that sing with motion and color. We urge you to refer to her books for detailed explanations of these methods of construction.

Today, Julie Luoma is the distributor of AnglePlay® products. If you need templates, patterns, etc. please visit her website: offthewallquilts.com.

Cutting with Templates

It is not difficult to cut shapes with acrylic templates. You may want to purchase some kind of sticky dots or adhesive for both sides of the templates if you have trouble with them sliding.

Julie Luoma recommends Ruler Magic, which is available on her website. A rotating cutting mat is also helpful when using templates.

You **MUST** cut multiple layers of fabric RIGHT SIDE UP because the templates have a left and right orientation depend-ing on which side of the template is facing up. For accuracy, we recommend cutting no more than four layers at a time. You will want to cut all three sides of the template rather than using the edge of the fabric to cut. Again, this just increases your precision when you stitch.

Block Trays

The concept of "block trays" is useful in AnglePlay®. Make a diagram of the block you are constructing by using paper and pencil to draw around the templates for a given block. As you cut fabric pieces, lay them on the corresponding shape on your block tray. You can then transfer the block tray to your sewing machine table and begin sewing.

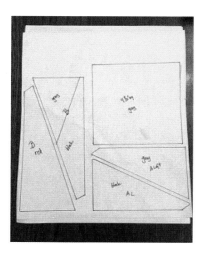

The order of construction for AnglePlay® blocks is as follows:
- Pieced triangles first
- Triangles into rectangles
- Rectangles sewn together

The patterns in this book are very detailed, with a picture for almost every step. You will soon get the hang of it and will be able to decipher any AnglePlay® block for piecing just by looking at the sample block picture.

Pieced Triangles

Pieced triangles are those in which a base triangle and side triangle are sewn from different fabrics and then cut again to the size of the entire template. Lines on each template show where the base and side triangles lie. There is a method for cutting base and side triangles that may be found in the following places:

- Instruction sheet included with templates
- On the web (offthewallquilts.com)
- Margaret J. Miller's books
- Classes at your local quilt shop

As of this printing, there is a Supplemental template set for templates A,B,C, and D that eliminates the need to use Margaret's original method for cutting pieced triangles. It is well worth the money to have this set as it is much faster and saves fabric.

Working with Stripes or Directional Fabric

One of the pleasures of making AnglePlay® quilts is that you begin to look at fabric differently. You may have stayed away from directional fabrics in the past, but stripes are particularly dynamic in AnglePlay® as are ombre fabrics. Stripes and ombre fabrics bring incredible motion to the designs.

When cutting triangles with stripes you can control the direction so that the stripes run either vertically or horizontally. Set the template in the direction you want the stripes to run.

If you are cutting half-square triangles place your ruler on point to get horizontal stripes.

If you are cutting quarter-square triangles you will get two triangles with horizontal stripes and two triangles with vertical stripes.

Making patterns simpler or more complex

Quilting, by nature, is a creative art. You are making the quilt so <u>you are in charge</u> of the design. With AnglePlay®, making alterations in the pattern is easy. If you do not want a pieced block, simply cut the shape with the entire template from the start. Alternately, if you want to divide a shape, make a pieced block where the pattern calls for a whole template.

We have included black and white diagrams for each pattern in the book. We encourage you to copy these and try coloring them in different ways. Often you can meld one block into another by strategic color placement. The alternate colorways presented in this book give examples of such "design decisions".

We purposely limited our color palettes in each pattern to simplify the look of the quilt. This does not mean that you cannot introduce many more colors or fabrics in these designs.

Some of the quilts are designed as square. Some quilters greatly prefer rectangular quilts. We hope that you personalize the square design to fit your preferences.

There are two easy ways to turn a square quilt into a rectangle:

- Add borders of different widths to increase the length more than width
- Add rows of blocks or elements already in the quilt to the top and bottom.

Reading our cutting charts

For each block in this book, we start with a cutting chart.

Example:

(1) Diagram Piece, Color		(2) # WOF Strips	(3) Template (# rectangles)	(4) Subcuts
A	Red	1 at 3-1/4"	A: 3-1/4" x 5" (6)	12 A left
HST	Yellow	1 at 4-7/8"	Squares 4-7/8" (6)	12 HST

Reading across the chart, (1) *Diagram Piece, color* is listed to help you identify where each fabric is placed in the block.

(2) *WOF* means width-of-fabric. This is the first cut you will make of each color.

(3) *Template (# rectangles)* tells you which AnglePlay® template is needed. We recommend cutting rectangles at the given size, then cutting the triangles with the specified template. The number in parentheses tells you how many rectangles you will need.

(4) *Subcuts* refers to the final piece that will be used in the block. The subcut could be a square, rectangle or an AnglePlay® triangle.

Let's get started!

As always we encourage you to follow our three E's:

ENJOY, EXPERIMENT and EXCEL!

Blossom Placemats

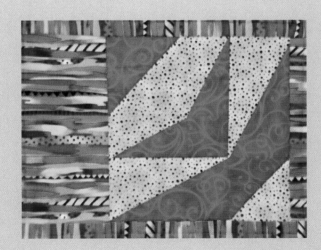

Blossom Placemats

11" x 15"
A & E templates

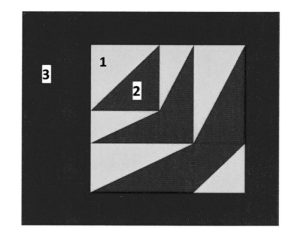

Fabric Requirements (for a set of 4)

1 – Tan	½ yd
2 – Green	½ yd
3 – Red border	½ yd

The placemats are made from a single block with borders of varying size.
Make each placemat unique by reversing the color placement in the block.

Blossom

9" blocks, make 4

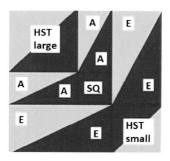

Diagram Piece, Color		# WOF Strips	Template (# rectangles)	Subcuts
HST (large)	Tan	1 at 4-7/8"	Squares 4-7/8" (2)	4 HST
	Green	1 at 4-7/8"	Squares 4-7/8" (2)	4 HST
HST (small)	Tan	** see note	Squares 3-7/8" (2)	4 HST
	Green		Squares 3-7/8" (2)	4 HST
A	Tan		A: 3-1/4" x 5" (4)	4 A right, 4 A left
	Green		A: 3-1/4" x 5" (4)	4 A right, 4 A left
E	Tan		E: 5-1/4" x 7" (4)	4 E right, 4 E left
	Green		E: 5-1/4" x 7" (4)	4 E right, 4 E left
SQ	Green		Squares 2-1/2" (4)	4 squares

** Note: you can cut different units from one strip. Start with the largest
width and work your way down to smaller pieces. Four placemats can be cut
from 2 WOF strips.

Sew the half square triangles.

Make 4 of the larger size (4-1/2")
 and 4 smaller (3-1/2").

Pair the A triangles and make 4 left facing and 4 right facing units.

4 left

4 right

Pair the E triangles and make 4 left facing and 4 right facing units.

4 left

4 right

Sew the left facing A unit the the right side of the larger HST.

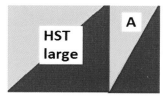

Sew the short end of the right facing A unit to the solid square of the same color.

Sew the A row to the bottom of the block.

Add the left facing E unit to the right side of the block.

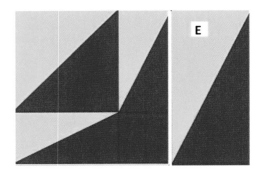

Sew the short end of the right facing E units to the smaller HST.

Sew this row on the bottom of the block. Make 4.

Borders

Cut a side border at 5-1/2" x 9-1/2".
Attach to block.

Cut another side border at 1-1/2" x 9-1/2".
Attach to opposite side.

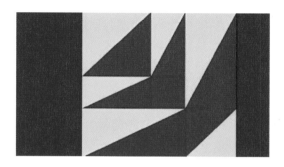

Cut the top and bottom borders 1-1/2" x 15".
Attach to block to finish placemat.

Quilt and finish as desired.
Visit TrueBlueQuilts.com for tutorials on finishing techniques.

Blossom Coloring Page

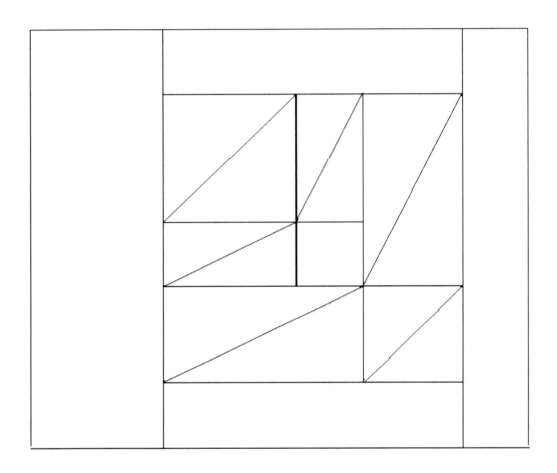

Thistles Table Runner

Thistles sample created by Helene Block

Thistles Table Runner

17" x 51"
A, B & G templates

Fabric Requirements

1 - Dark green	½ yd	4 - Light purple	¼ yd
2 - Med green	½ yd	5 - Dark Purple	¼ yd
3 - Light green	¼ yd		

Star in a Knot
12-1/2" blocks, make 3

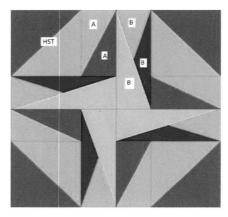

Diagram Piece, Color		# WOF Strips	Template (# rectangles)	Subcuts
HST	Dark Purple	1 at 4-7/8"	Squares 4-7/8" (6)	12 HST
	Med Green	1 at 4-7/8"	Squares 4-7/8" (6)	12 HST
A	Dark Purple	1 at 3-1/4"	A: 3-1/4" x 5" (6)	12 A left
	Med Green	1 at 3-1/4"	A: 3-1/4" x 5" (6)	12 A left
B	Light Purple	1 at 7"	B: 3-1/4" x 7" (6)	12 B right
	Med Green*	1 at 5"	B_base: 3-1/2" x 5" (12)*	12 B base
	Dark Green*	3 at 2"	B_side: 2" x 8" (12)*	12 B side

* Use the supplementary templates to cut partial units for pieced triangles

Pair the dark purple and medium green triangles and sew into HST. Make 12. Trim to 4-1/2".

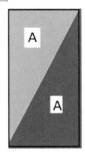

Pair the dark purple and medium green A left facing triangles. Sew into rectangles. Make 12.

Pair the medium green B base triangles with the dark green side triangles. Sew on the right side of the side triangle and trim using the B template.

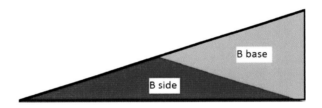

Pair the B partial to the light purple B right facing triangles. Sew into rectangles. Make 12.

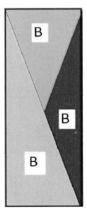

Sew the A units to the HST as shown. Make 12.

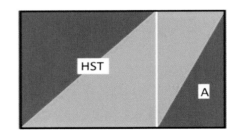

Sew the B units to the bottom of the HST-A units as shown. Make 12.

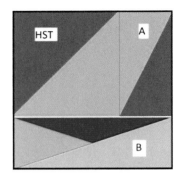

This is one quadrant of the Star in a Knot block. Arrange 4 quadrants to form the star and piece the block. Make 3.

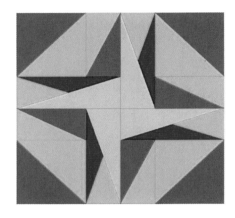

Setting Triangles

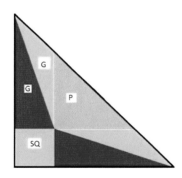

Diagram Piece, Color		# WOF Strips	Template (# rectangles)	Subcuts
SQ	Light green	1 at 3-1/2"	Squares 3-1/2" (4)	4 squares
G	Dark green	1 at 4-1/4"	G: 4-1/4" x 10" (4)	4 G right and 4 G left
	Light green	1 at 4-1/4"	G: 4-1/4" x 10" (4)	4 G right and 4 G left
P	Light purple	1 at 7"	Squares 7" (2)	4 HST

Pair the light and dark green G units and sew into rectangles. Make 4 right facing and 4 left facing units.

Right facing

Left facing

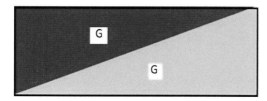

Sew the light purple triangles to the light green side of the right facing units as shown. Make 4.

Excess fabric will be trimmed when the quilt is assembled.

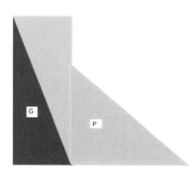

Sew the small light green squares to the short, dark
green end of the left facing units as shown. Make 4.

Sew the two pieces to form the setting triangles. Excess fabric will be trimmed after quilt is fully assembled.

Sew the Thistles table runner together in three rows. Sew a setting triangle to the left side of a block.

Sew two setting triangles to the middle block, changing the orientation on either side as shown.

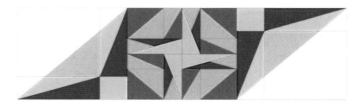

Sew a setting triangle to the right side of the third block.

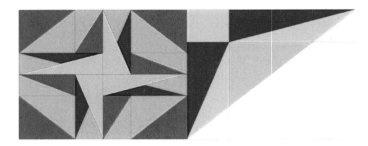

Sew the diagonal rows together as shown. Trim the excess fabric so the sides are straight.

Quilt and finish as desired.

Thistles Coloring Page

Joyful Noise
Table Runner

Joyful Noise
17" x 62"
A, B & H templates

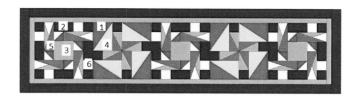

Fabric Requirements

1 - Red	1/3 yd	4 - Yellow	¼ yd
2 - Dark Green * includes borders	2/3 yd	5 - Light Green	2/3 yd
3 - Gold * includes borders	2/3 yd	6 - White	1/3 yd

Dune Grass
12-1/2" blocks, make 3
B template

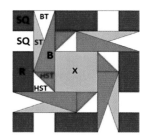

Diagram Piece, Color		# WOF Strips	Template (# rectangles)	Subcuts
SQ	Dark Green	1 at 2-1/2"	N/A	12 2-1/2" squares
	White	1 at 2-1/2"	N/A	12 2-1/2" squares
R	Dark Green	2 at 2-1/2"	Rectangles 4-1/2" (12)	12 rectangles 2-1/2" x 4-1/2"
HST	Red	1 at 2-7/8"	Squares 2-7/8" (6)	12 HST
	White	1 at 2-7/8"	Squares 2-7/8 (6)	12 HST
X	Gold	1 at 4-1/2"	N/A	3 4-1/2" squares
B	Light Green	2 at 3-1/4"	B: 3-1/4" x 7" (6)	12 B left
	Gold	2 at 3-1/4"	B_side: 3-1/4" x 7" (12)	12 B side
	White	1 at 3-1/4"	B_base: 3-1/4"x4-1/4" (12)	12 B base

Construct pieced triangles using the Gold side triangles and White Base triangles. Make 12.

Attach the partials to the Green B triangles to make 12 rectangle units.

Sew the red and white HST together to make a square unit. Make 12.

Sew the green and white squares together, then add a Green R unit to make a long strip.

Add the B units and HST to complete one quadrant of the block.

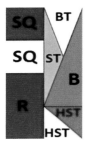

The Dune Grass block is sewn together using partial seams to attach the quadrants around the center square.

Begin with gold X square and one quadrant, and sew from the center of the gold square to the end of the seam.

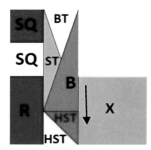

Add another quadrant along the bottom edge.

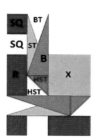

Continue with the third quadrant on the right.

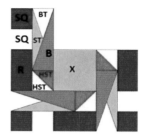

Sew the fourth quadrant into place, then finish the seam from the first quadrant.

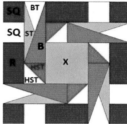

Make 3 blocks.

Prop Plane
12-1/2"" blocks, make 2
A & H templates

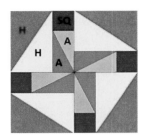

Diagram Piece, Color		# WOF Strips	Template (#rectangles)	Subcuts
H	Red	1 at 5-1/4"	H: 5-1/4" x 7" (4)	8 H left
	Yellow	1 at 5-1/4"	H: 5-1/4" x 7" (4)	8 H left
SQ	Dark Green	1 at 2-1/2"	Squares 2-1/2" (8)	8 2-1/2" squares
A	Gold	1 at 3-1/4"	A: 3-1/4" x 5" (4)	8 A right
	Light Green	1 at 3-1/4"	A: 3-1/4" x 5" (4)	8 A right

Pair the red and yellow H units and sew into rectangles. Make 8.

Pair the gold and (light) green A units and sew into rectangles. Make 8.

Sew the dark green squares to the gold end of the A unit. Attach to the yellow side of the H units. Make 8.

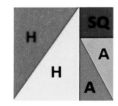

Sew 4 quadrants into a block. Make 2.

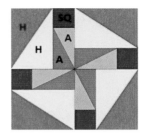

As shown in the photographs, changing the H units to solid fabric gives the Prop Plane block a modern feel.

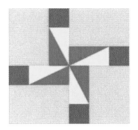

Alternate Dune Grass and Prop Plane blocks to construct the center of the table runner.

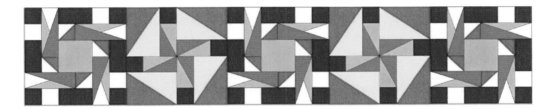

Borders (optional)

Inner border (gold) – cut four 1" strips. Cut 2 strips at 12-1/2"" and attach to short ends. Cut 2 strips at 61-1/2" and attach to the sides.

Outer border (green) – cut four 2-1/2" strips. Cut 2 strips at 13-1/2" and attach to short ends. Cut 2 strips at 65-1/2" for the sides.

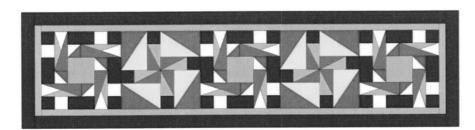

Quilt and finish as desired.

Joyful Noise Coloring Page

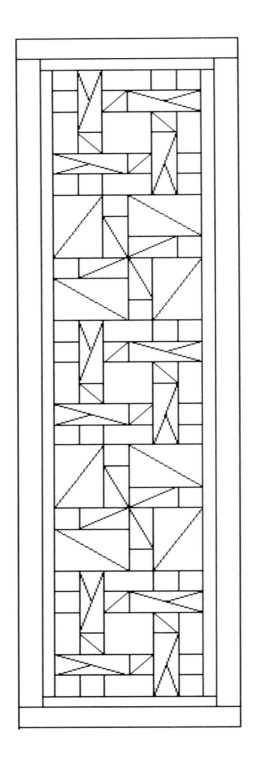

Fruit Salad

Fruit Salad
56" square
A template

Use a progression of colors, carrying one color from the center of one ring to the outside of the next ring.

Fabric Requirements

1 - Red	¼ yd
2 - Yellow	½ yd
3 - Green	7/8 yd
4 - Purple	2/3 yd
5 - White	1.5 yd

Diagram Piece, Color		# WOF Strips	Template (# rectangles)	Subcuts
A	Red	2 at 3-1/4"	A: 3-1/4" x 5" (12)	12 A right, 12 A left
	Yellow	5 at 3-1/4"	A: 3-1/4" x 5" (40)	40 A right, 40 A left
	Green	9 at 3-1/4"	A: 3-1/4" x 5" (72)	72 A right, 72 A left
	Purple	6 at 3-1/4"	A: 3-1/4" x 5" (44)	44 A right, 44 A left
Solid Borders	White	1 at 8-1/2"	1 square 8-1/2"	1 square 8-1/2"
	White	9 at 4-1/2"	Border strips as needed	Subcut strips: 2 @ 17", 2 @ 24-3/4", 2 @ 32-3/4", 2 @ 40-3/4", 2 @ 49-1/4", 2 @ 57-1/4"

Sew rectangles by pairing the right-facing triangles together. Repeat with the left-facing triangles.

With red+yellow, make 12 pairs each.
With yellow+green, make 28 pairs each.
With green+purple, make 44 pairs each.

Use 4 rectangles (2 of each orientation) to make the full diamond unit.

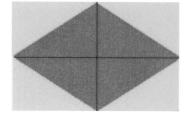

With red+yellow, make 6 full units.
With yellow+green, make 14 full units.
With green+purple, make 22 full units.

Piece the quilt by adding diamond units to the sides first, and then the top and bottom of each ring.

Round 1 - Start by adding a red+yellow diamond to each side of the white square.

Sew the remaining diamond units in pairs, end to end.

Add the paired units to the top and bottom of the white square.

Round 2 – Attach the 17" white strips to the left and right sides of the quilt top.

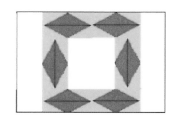

Note: It is always good practice to measure your quilt before adding borders. Individual machines and seam allowances differ, so measure and cut borders to your specific size!

Add the 24-3/4" strips to the top and bottom to complete the ring.

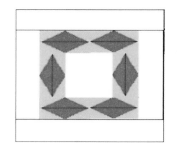

Round 3 – Sew 3 yellow+green diamonds together to form a side row. Make 2.

Attach to the sides of the quilt top.

Sew the remaining yellow+green diamonds in rows of 4. Make 2.

Attach to the top and bottom of the quilt top.

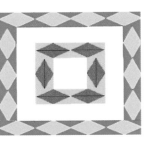

Round 4 – Attach the 32-3/4" white strips to the left and right sides of the quilt top.

Add the 40-3/4" strips to the top and bottom to complete the ring.

Round 5 – Sew 5 green+purple diamonds together to form a side row. Make 2.

Attach to the sides of the quilt top.

Sew the remaining green+purple diamonds in rows of 6. Make 2.

Attach to the top and bottom of the quilt top.

Round 6 - Attach the 49-1/4" white strips to the left and right sides of the quilt top. Add the 57-1/4" strips to the top and bottom to complete the ring.

Quilt and finish as desired.

Fruit Salad Coloring Page

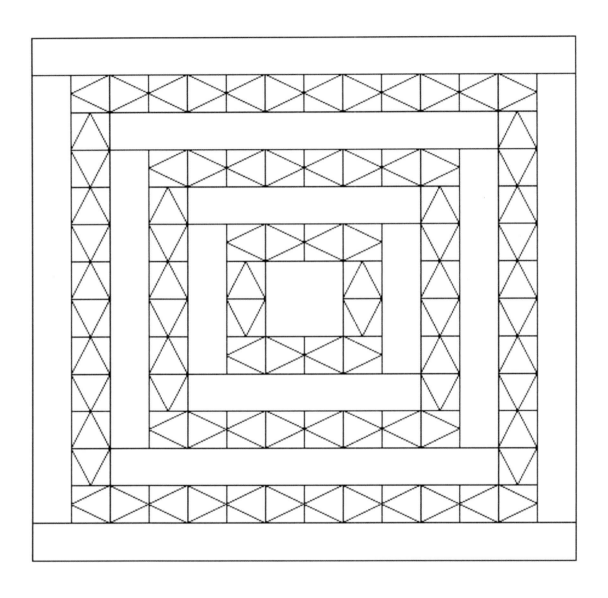

Two By Two

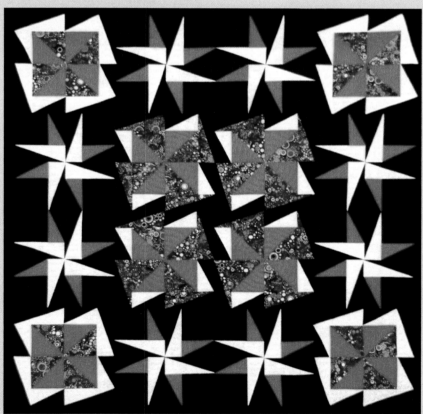

Two by Two sample created by Ann Beam

Two by Two
Size50" square
A & B templates

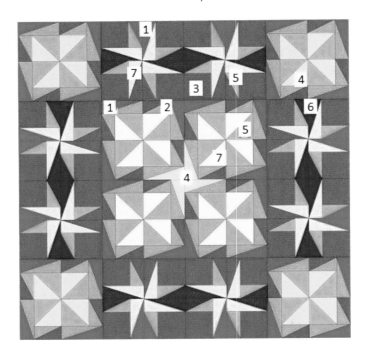

Fabric Requirements

1 - Teal	1 yd	5 - Light Green	1 yd
2 - Purple	¾ yd	6 - Dark Green	¾ yd
3 - Brown	1 – 1/4 yd	7 -White	1 yd
4 - Yellow	½ yd		

The four center Square Dance blocks have a different color pinwheel than the four corner blocks. One outer triangle is a different color to create the center star. Change colors of any component to give your quilt a different feel, like the red and black quilt shown on the previous page.

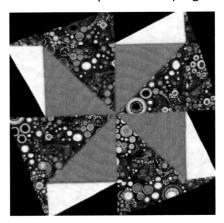

Square Dance
12-1/2" blocks
A & B templates

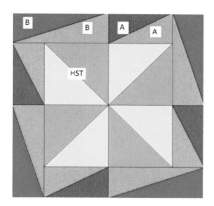
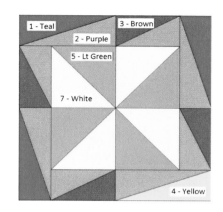

Diagram Piece, Color		# WOF Strips	Template (# rectangles)	Subcuts
HST	Light Green	2 at 4-7/8"	Squares 4-7/8" (16)	32 HST
	Yellow	1 at 4-7/8"	Squares 4-7/8" (8)	16 HST
	White	1 at 4-7/8"	Squares 4-7/8" (8)	16 HST
A	Purple	2 at 3-1/4"	A: 3-1/4" x 5" (16)	32 A right
	Brown	2 at 3-1/4"	A: 3-1/4" x 5" (16)	32 A right
B	Purple	3 at 3-1/4"	B: 3-1/4" x 7" (16)	32 B right
	Yellow	1 at 3-1/4"	B: 3-1/4" x 7" (2)	4 B right
	Teal	3 at 3-1/4"	B: 3-1/4" x 7" (14)	28 B right

Sew the two types of HST units by pairing 16 green with 16 yellow,

and 16 green with 16 white.

Sew the A units by pairing 32 purple with 32 brown.

Sew the B triangles into rectangles.
Make 4 with purple and yellow.
Make 28 with purple and teal.

Sew the A units with the green and yellow HST.

Add the purple and teal B unit to form the corner quadrants as shown, then join into the finished block.

Make 4 corner blocks.

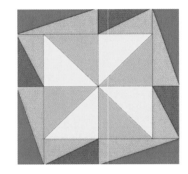

For the center blocks, sew the white HST to the A units.

Add the B units. Make 12 quadrants with the purple and teal,

and 4 quadrants with the yellow and purple.

Make 4 center blocks as shown.

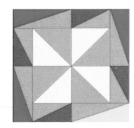

Kingfisher blocks
12-1/2" blocks
A & B templates

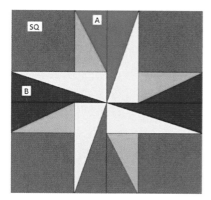

Diagram Piece, Color		# WOF Strips	Template (# rectangles)	Subcuts
SQ	Brown	4 at 4-1/2"	Squares 4-1/2"	32 squares 4-1/2"
A	Light Green	2 at 3-1/4"	A: 3-1/4" x 5" (16)	32 A right
	Dark Green	1 at 3-1/4"	A: 3-1/4" x 5" (8)	16 A right
	Teal	1 at 3-1/4"	A: 3-1/4" x 5" (4)	8 A right
	Brown	1 at 3-1/4"	A: 3-1/4" x 5" (4)	8 A right
B	White	3 at 3-1/4"	B: 3-1/4" x 7" (16)	32 B left
	Dark Green	2 at 3-1/4"	B: 3-1/4" x 7" (8)	16 B left
	Teal	1 at 3-1/4"	B: 3-1/4" x 7" (4)	8 B left
	Brown	1 at 3-1/4"	B: 3-1/4" x 7" (4)	8 B left

Make 8 rectangles with light green and brown A triangles.

Make 8 rectangles with light green and teal A triangles.

Make 16 rectangles with the light green and dark green A triangles.

Make 8 rectangles with white and brown B triangles.

Make 8 rectangles with white and teal B triangles.

Make 16 rectangles with white and dark green B triangles.

Add a brown square to each of the A rectangles.

Make 4 with the light green and brown units.

Make 8 with the light green and dark green units.

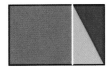

Make 4 with the light green and teal units.

Add the B units to make the block quadrants.

Make 4 with the dark green/white B units and the light green/brown A units.

Make 4 with the brown/white B units and the light green/dark green A units.

Make 4 with the teal/white B units and the light green/dark green A units.
Make 4 with the dark green/white B units and the teal/light green A units.

Layout the blocks according to the diagram and sew rows to assemble the quilt top.

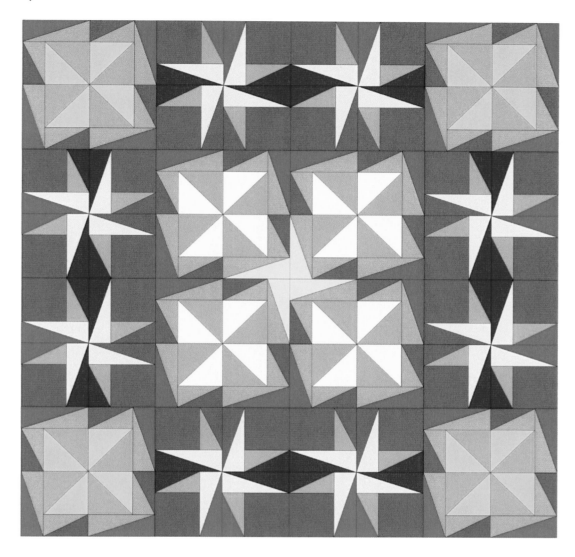

Quilt and finish as desired.

Two By Two Coloring Page

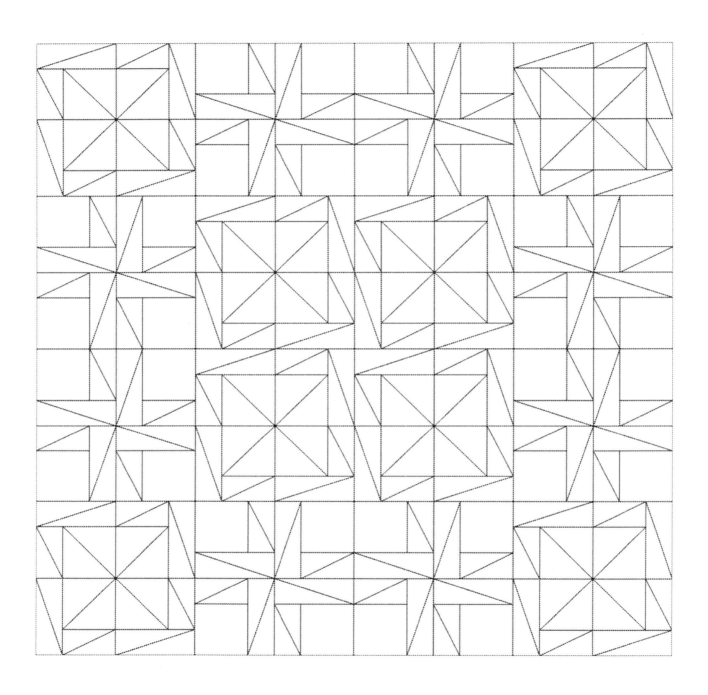

Birds
Flying
High

Birds Flying High
size 48" x 60"
B & K templates

Fabric Requirements

1 – White	½ yd	4 – Purple	7/8 yd
2 – Cream	1-2/3 yd	5 – Black	1 yd
3 – Orange (stripe)	½ yd	6 - Red	3/8 yd

Ann's Plan (variation)
12" finished - Make 10
B & K templates

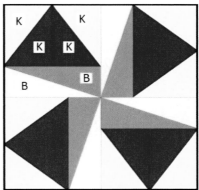

Diagram Piece, Color		# WOF Strips	Template (# rectangles)	Subcuts
K1	Cream	1 at 4-3/4"	K: 3-1/4"x4-3/4" (40)	40 K1 (top) right 40 K1 (top) left
	Purple	1 at 4-3/4"	K: 3-1/4"x4-3/4" (40)	40 K1 (top) right 40 K1 (top) left
B	Orange	4 at 3-1/4"	B: 3-1/4" x 7" (20)	40 B left
	White	4 at 3-1/4"	B: 3-1/4" x 7" (20)	40 B left

Pair the K1 triangles together to make rectangles. Sew 40 of each as shown.

Right facing   Left facing

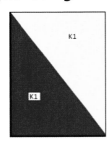   

Sew the K1 units together along the purple edge as shown.
Make 40.

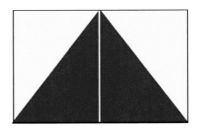

Sew the B triangles together to make rectangles.
Make 40.

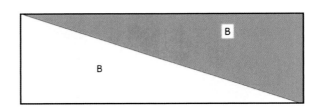

Sew the orange side of the B rectangle to the purple side of the K unit. This forms one quadrant of the Ann's Plan block. Make 40.

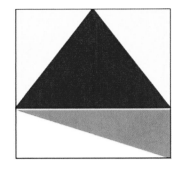

Put four quadrants together and rotate the units to form the pinwheel. Sew into full blocks. Make 10.

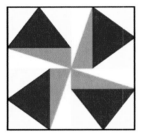

Ribbon Border
12-1/2" finished
Make 10

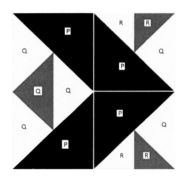

Diagram Piece, Color		# WOF Strips	Subcuts
P	Black	4 at 6-7/8"	20 squares 6-7/8" cut once on diagonal to make 40 HST
Q	Red	1 at 7-1/4"	5 squares 7-1/4" cut twice on diagonal to make 10 QST
	Cream	3 at 7-1/4"	13 squares 7-1/4" cut twice on diagonal to make 50 QST
R	Red	1 at 3-7/8"	10 squares 3-7/8" cut once on diagonal to make 20 HST
	Cream	1 at 3-7/8"	10 squares 3-7/8" cut once on diagonal to make 20 HST

Pair 10 Red and 10 Cream large Q triangles and sew
along the diagonal to form half square triangles.
Make 10 HST units.

Sew the short side of 2 Q cream triangles to the red
sides of the HST unit to form the large triangle
section of the block. Make 10.

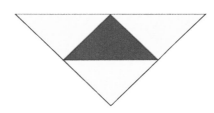

Add 2 of the P black HST to each side of the large
triangle section to form the top half of the block.
Make 10 and set aside.

Sew the small R cream and red triangles together along a short edge to form
a two color triangle.
There are two versions...make 10 of each.
Red on the right   Red on the left

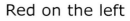

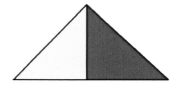

Add the remaining Q cream triangles along the red edge of the previous unit
as shown. Make 10 of each.
Red on the right   Red on the left

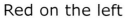

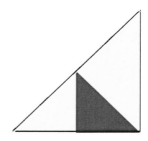
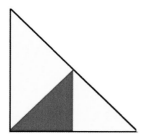

Add the remaining black P triangles to the previous unit to form squares. Trim to 6-1/2".

Sew these squares together along the black side.

Join the two rows together to finish the Ribbon Border block.
Make 10.

Layout the blocks in straight rows as shown in the diagram.

The photographs show an alternate layout with additional Ribbon Border blocks. This version of the quilt uses 9 Ann's Plan (variation) blocks with 16 Ribbon Border blocks.

Quilt and finish as desired.

Birds Flying High Coloring Page

Alternate Birds Flying High
Coloring Page

Race Is On

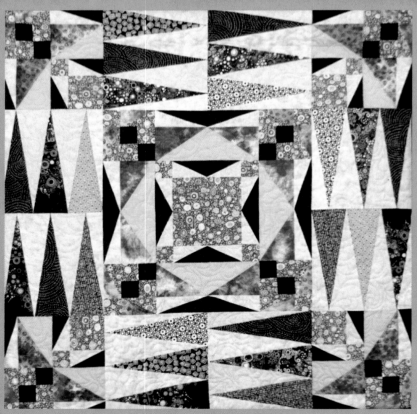

Race Is On sample created by Michelle Kessler

Race is On
48" x 48"
A, B, & H templates
Paper Piecing

Fabric Requirements

1 - Teal	1/3 yd
2 – Dark Grey	½ yd
3 – Light Grey	1-2/3 yd
4 - Green	1-1/4 yd
5 - Yellow	¼ yd
6 - Pink	1/3 yd

Dogtooth
12-1/2" block
Paper piecing

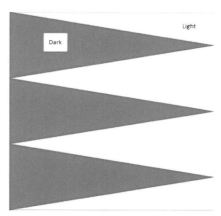

Diagram color	# WOF Strips	Subcuts
Light	5 at 3"	16 rectangles 3" x 13-1/2"
	5 at 5-1/2"	16 rectangles 5-1/2" x 13-1/2"
Dark	8 at 5-1/2"	24 rectangles 5-1/2" x 13-1/2"

Print Dogtooth pattern from page 60 for paper piecing. Enlarge 200%.
Alternate light and dark strips as indicated on the pattern pieces.

Swallowtail
12-1/2" Block
A, B & H templates

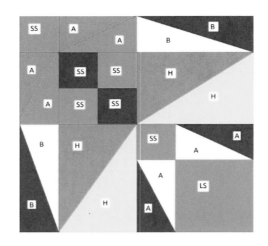

Diagram Piece, Color		# WOF Strips	Template (# rectangles)	Subcuts
SS	Teal	2 at 2-1/2"	Squares 2-1/2" (32)	32 squares 2-1/2"
	Dark Grey	1 at 2-1/2"	Squares 2-1/2" (16)	16 squares 2-1/2"
A	Teal	1 at 3-1/4"	A: 3-1/4" x 5" (8)	8 A right 8 A left
	Pink	1 at 3-1/4"	A: 3-1/4" x 5" (8)	8 A right 8 A left
	Light Grey	1 at 3-1/4"	A: 3-1/4" x 5" (8)	8 A right 8 A left
	Dark Grey	1 at 3-1/4"	A: 3-1/4" x 5" (8)	8 A right 8 A left
B	Dark Grey	2 at 3-1/4"	B: 3-1/4" x 7" (8)	8 B right 8 B left
	Light Grey	2 at 3-1/4"	B: 3-1/4" x 7" (8)	8 B right 8 B left
H	Pink	2 at 5-1/4"	H: 5-1/4" x 7" (8)	8 H right 8 H left
	Yellow	2 at 5-1/4"	H: 5-1/4" x 7" (8)	8 H right 8 H left

Pair the A triangles and sew into rectangles. Make 8 of each.
Right Facing Units   Left Facing Units

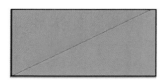

Sew 8 small teal squares to the pink end of the right facing units. Make 8.

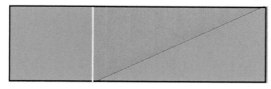

Sew 16 small teal squares to the small grey squares to form 4-patches.
Make 8.

Sew the teal side of the left-facing units to one side of the 4-patch (with the grey square in the upper left as shown). Make 8.

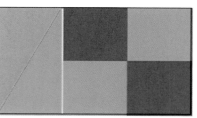

Sew the A units together to form the first quadrant of the Swallowtail block. Make 8 and set aside.

Pair the B triangles and sew into rectangles. Make 8 of each.
Right Facing Units   Left Facing Units

Pair the H triangles and sew into rectangles. Make 8 of each.
Right Facing Units   Left Facing Units

Sew the light grey side of the B left facing units to the pink side of the H right facing units as shown. Make 8.

Repeat with the left facing units as shown. Make 8.

Pair the grey A triangles and sew into rectangles. Make 8 of each.
Right Facing Units   Left Facing Units

   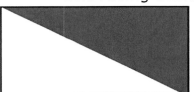

Sew 8 small teal squares to the light grey side of the left-facing A units. Make 8.

Sew the light grey side of the right-facing A units to the large teal squares. Make 8.

Sew the two grey/teal units together to complete the last quadrant as shown. Make 8.

Assemble the four quadrants as shown to complete the Swallowtail block. Make 8.

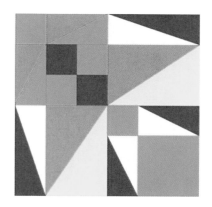

Assemble the quilt in rows according to the diagram.

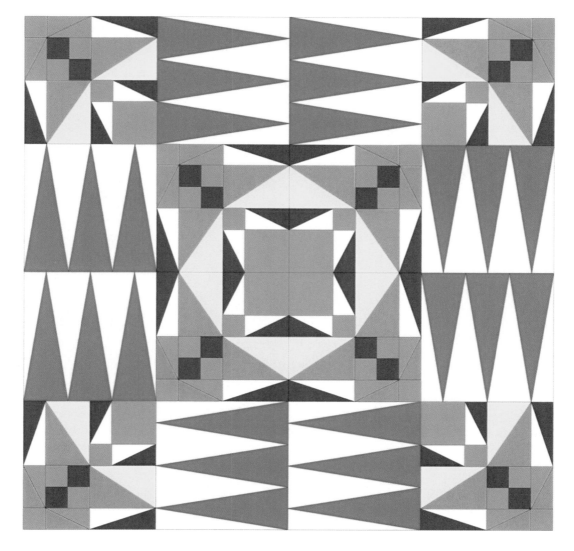

Quilt and finish as desired.

Dogtooth Foundation Pattern

Enlarge 200% for a 12" Block

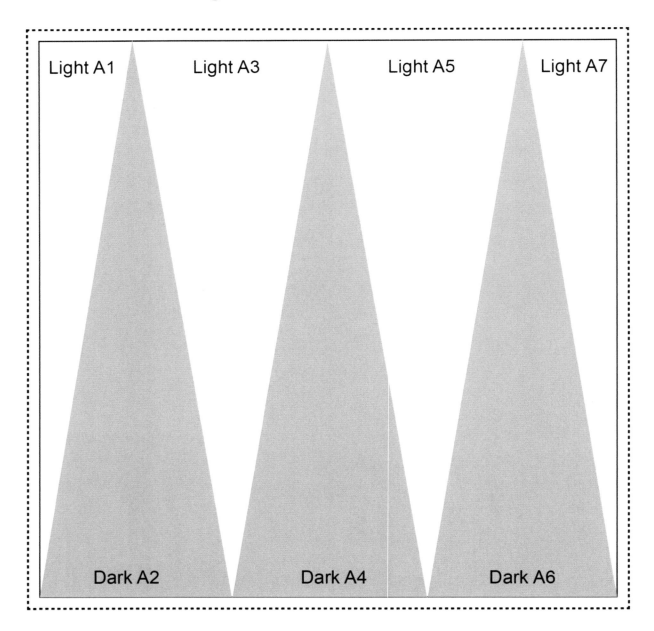

Race Is On Coloring Page

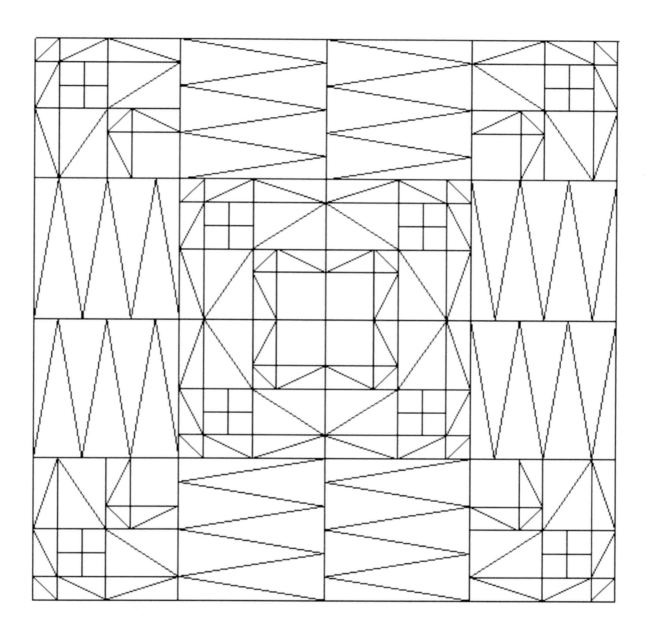

Around the Pond

Around the Pond
38" x 50"
A & G templates

Fabric Requirements

1 – Background	1 yd	6 – Bright Yellow	1/3 yd
2 – Orange	2/3 yd	7 – Muted Yellow	1/2 yd
3 – Green	1-1/4 yd	8 – Red	1 yd
4 – Brown	2/3 yd	9 – Pale Green	1 yd
5 – Medium Brown	2/3 yd		

Dresden Blade
12-1/2" blocks, make 4
Applique

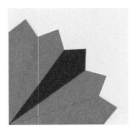

Cut four 13" squares of background fabric. Cut the blades with the paper templates on page 68. You will need 4 of Blade 1, 8 of Blade 2 and 8 of Blade 3. Sew the fan blades along the long edge then machine applique the blades onto the background square, with Blade 1 in the center of each fan.

Merry Go Round
12-1/2" blocks

Center blocks – Make 10   Corner blocks – make 4

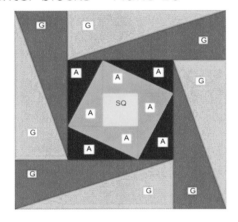
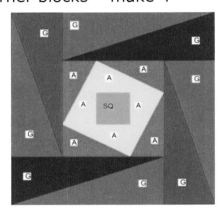

Diagram piece, color		# WOF Strips	Template (# rectangles)	Subcuts
SQ	Yellow	1 at 2-1/2"	Squares 2-1/2" (10)	10 squares 2-1/2"
	Gold	1 at 2-1/2"	Squares 2-1/2" (4)	4 squares 2-1/2"
A	Gold	3 at 3-1/4"	A: 3-1/4" x 5" (20)	40 A left
	Brown	3 at 3-1/4"	A: 3-1/4" x 5" (20)	40 A left
	Yellow	2 at 3-1/4"	A: 3-1/4" x 5" (8)	16 A left
	Dark orange	2 at 3-1/4"	A: 3-1/4" x 5" (8)	16 A left
G	Tan	3 at 10"	G: 4-1/4" x 10" (20)	40 G right
	Red	3 at 10"	G: 4-1/4" x 10" (20)	40 G right
	Green	1 at 4-1/4"	G: 4-1/4" x 10" (4)	8 G right
	Brown	1 at 4-1/4"	G: 4-1/4" x 10" (4)	8 G right
	Rust	2 at 4-1/4"	G: 4-1/4" x 10" (8)	16 G right

Sew the A units together. Make 40 gold with brown, and 16 yellow with dark orange.

Sew the G units together. Make 40 tan with red, 8 green with rust, and 8 brown with rust.

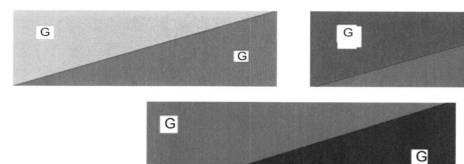

Assemble the blocks by sewing rectangles around the center square, using partial seams.

Step 1: sew halfway down the first seam.

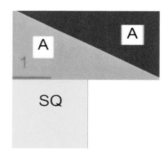

Steps 2 – 4: sew the other three rectangles on the remaining sides of the center square.

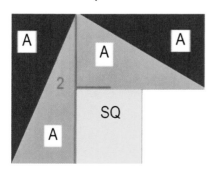 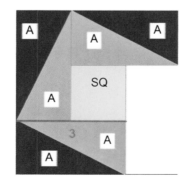 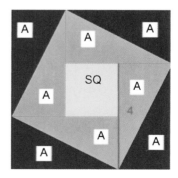

Step 5: Finish the seam that was partially sewn in step 1

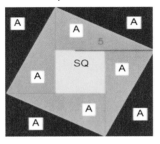

Finish the block by repeating the partial seams with the G rectangles.

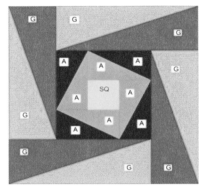

Around the Pond uses an on-point layout. Sew the two-color setting triangles before sewing the blocks into rows.

Setting triangles

Fabric 1 matches the background of the Dresden Blade blocks. Cut 5 squares at 7-7/8", then cut once on the diagonal to make 10 HST.

Fabric 2 matches the green fabric from the Dresden Blade 2. Cut 5 strips at 4-1/2", and sub-cut into 19-1/2" strips.

Sew the HST to the rectangle.

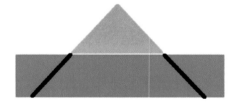

Trim the sides using the 45-degree marks on a ruler, aligned with the base of the rectangle.

Corner triangles

Cut 2 squares at 11-7/8", then cut once on the diagonal to make 4 HST.

Assemble quilt top in diagonal rows according to the diagram.

Quilt and finish as desired.

Dresden Blade Template

Enlarge 200%

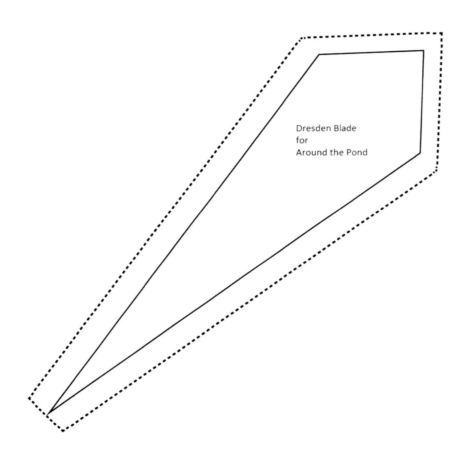

Dresden Blade
for
Around the Pond

Around the Pond Coloring Page

Ripples

Once you have experience with AnglePlay® quilts, use this pattern to increase your skills!
If you are exhausted after the sheer number of pieces in the center, take a break and use plain corner and setting triangles instead of the version shown here.

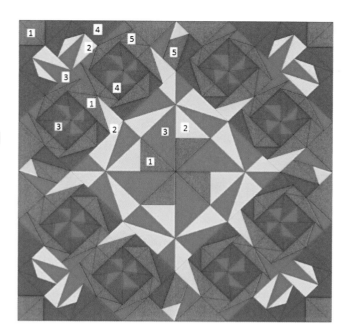

Ripples
50" x 50"
A, B, E, H, I & K templates

Fabric Requirements

1 - Pink	1-1/2 yd		4 - Blue	1-1/4 yd
2 - Peach	2/3 yd		5 - Orange	1/2 yd
3 - Green	1-1/8 yd			

Twinkle Toes blocks
12-1/2" block, make 4
I template

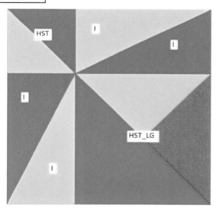

Diagram piece, color		# WOF Strips	Template (# rectangles)	Subcuts
HST_LG	Green	1 at 9-1/4"	Squares 9-1/4" (2)	4 HST
	Peach	1 at 6-7/8"	Squares 6-7/8" (2)	4 HST
	Pink	1 at 6-7/8"	Squares 6-7/8" (2)	4 HST
I	Green	1 at 5-1/4"	I: 5-1/4" x 9" (4)	4 I right, 4 I left
	Peach	1 at 5-1/4"	I: 5-1/4" x 9" (4)	4 I right, 4 I left
HST	Green	*1 at 2-1/2"	Squares 2-1/2" (2)	4 HST
	Peach	*1 at 2-1/2"	Squares 2-1/2" (2)	4 HST

*Note: use leftover pieces to cut smaller strips

Begin with the larger HST. Sew the peach and pink HST together on a short side to form half of the HST.
Make 4.

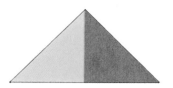

Add the green HST to form a square.
Make 4.

Sew the I peach and green triangles together to form rectangles.
Make 4 left facing   and 4 right facing.

With the smaller green and peach triangles, make 4 HST.

Sew the green side of the small HST to the peach side of the I right-facing rectangle.

Sew the peach side of the I left-facing rectangle to the green side of the large HST_LG.

Then assemble the Twinkle Toes block. Make 4

Weather Vane Block
12-1/2"– Make 8
A, B, E, H, K Templates

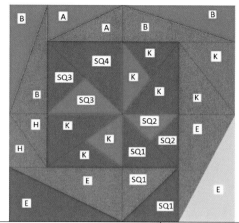

Diagram Piece, Color		# WOF Strips	Template (# rectangles)	Subcuts
A	Pink	1 at 3-1/4"	A: 3-1/4" x 5" (4)	8 A right
	Green	1 at 3-1/4"	A: 3-1/4" x 5" (4)	8 A right
B	Pink	2 at 3-1/4"	B: 3-1/4" x 7" (8)	16 B left
	Green	2 at 3-1/4"	B: 3-1/4" x 7" (8)	16 B left
K	Pink	1 at 5"	K1: 3-1/4" x 5 (4)	8 K1 (top) right
	Orange	1 at 5"	K1: 3-1/4" x 5 (4)	8 K1 (top) right
	Blue	1 at 5"	K1: 3-1/4" x 5 (8)	8 K1 (top) right 8 K1 (top) left
	Green	1 at 3"	Rectangles not needed	8 K1 side, 8 K1 base
	Blue	1 at 3"	Rectangles not needed	8 K1 side, 8 K1 base
E	Pink	2 at 4-1/4"	E: 4-1/4" x 7" (8)	16 E left
	Peach	1 at 4-1/4"	E: 4-1/4" x 7" (4)	8 E left
	Blue	1 at 4-1/4"	E: 4-1/4" x 7" (4)	8 E left
SQ1	Blue	1 at 3-7/8"	Square 3-7/8" (8)	16 HST
	Pink	1 at 3-7/8"	Square 3-7/8" (4)	8 HST
H	Pink	1 at 3"	H1: 3" x 4" (4)	8 H1 (top) right
	Orange	1 at 3"	H1: 3" x 4" (4)	8 H1 (top) right
SQ2	Green	*1 at 4-1/4"	Square 4-1/4" (2)	8 QST
	Blue	*1 at 4-1/4"	Square 4-1/4" (2)	8 QST
SQ3	Green	*1 at 5-1/4"	Square 5-1/4" (2)	8 QST
	Blue	*1 at 5-1/4"	Square 5-1/4" (2)	8 QST
SQ4	Blue	*1 at 4-7/8"	Square 4-7/8" (4)	8 HST

*Note: use the leftover pieces from SQ3 to cut SQ2 and SQ4

Sew the pink and green A triangles into rectangles.
Make 8.

Sew the pink and green B triangles into rectangles.
Make 16.

Sew two green and blue SQ3 triangles together on a short side according to the diagram. Keep the green triangle on the left side.

Add the blue SQ4 triangle on the long side to create a square. Make 8.

Sew the A units on top of the blue and green square, then add the B rectangle to the left side to complete the top left quadrant. Make 8.

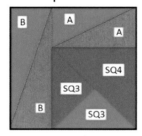

Construct the blue and green pieced K triangles.
Make 8 of each colorway, as shown:
Blue side and green base   Green side and blue base

Sew a blue K1 left-facing triangle on the long edge of the pieced triangle with the green side to create a square.

Sew the orange and pink K1 right-facing triangles into rectangles.
Make 8.

Sew the pink side of the K1 unit to the blue side of the square, then add the pink and green B units to form the top right quadrant. Make 8.

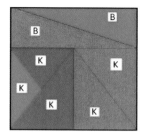

Sew a blue K1 right-facing triangle to the long edge of the remaining pieced triangles with the blue side. Make 8.

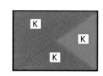

Sew the pink and orange H1 triangles into rectangles. Make 8.

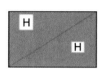

Sew the pink side of the H unit to the short end of the blue and green square.

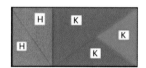

Sew the pink and blue E triangles into rectangles. Make 8.

Add the E rectangles to the H+K units to finish the Bottom Left quadrant. Make 8.

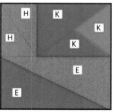

Sew the blue and green SQ2 triangles together on the short side. Keep the green to the left side. Make 8.

Sew 8 of the blue SQ1 triangles on the long side to form a square.

Sew the remaining blue and the pink SQ1 triangles to form a square. Make 8.

Sew these two squares together with the pink in the middle as shown.

Sew the pink and peach E triangles into rectangles. Make 8.

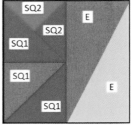

Sew the pink side of the E units to the square section to finish the bottom right quadrant.

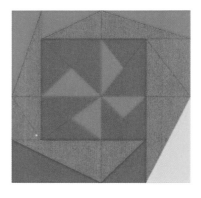

Sew the four quadrants together to create the finished block. Make 8.

Unplugged
8" blocks
E template
Make 8 in one colorway (Diagram P)   Make 4 in the 2nd colorway (Diagram Q)

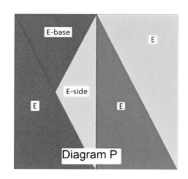

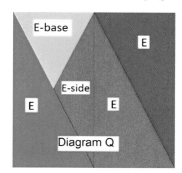

Diagram Piece, Color		# WOF Strips	Template (# rectangles)	Subcuts
E	Blue	1 at 4-1/4"	E: 4-1/4" x 7" (6)	12 E right
	Green	1 at 4-1/4"	E: 4-1/4" x 7" (6)	12 E right
	Peach	1 at 4-1/4"	E: 4-1/4" x 7" (4)	8 E right
	Orange	1 at 4-1/4"	E: 4-1/4" x 7" (2)	4 E right
E-base	Blue	1 at 4"	*Rectangles not needed*	8 E base
	Peach	1 at 4"	*Rectangles not needed*	4 E base
E-side	Peach	2 at 2"	*Rectangles not needed*	8 E side
	Orange	1 at 2"	*Rectangles not needed*	4 E side

Sew the blue base triangles to the right side of the peach side triangles.

Sew the blue E triangle to the pieced triangle with the blue base.
Sew the green and peach E triangles into rectangles.
Finish the Unplugged unit according to Diagram P. Make 8.

Repeat with the colors for Diagram Q.

Sew the peach base triangles to the right side of the orange side triangles.
Sew the green E triangle to the pieced triangle with the peach base.
Sew the orange and blue E triangles into rectangles.
Finish the Unplugged unit according to Diagram Q. Make 4.

Cutting for the corner squares and setting triangles:

Color	(Number), Size, Shape
Pink corner	(4) 4-1/2" squares
Blue corner	(4) 4-7/8" squares, 8 HST
Blue sides	(4) 7" squares, 8 HST
Pink sides	(4) 7" squares, 8 HST

For the setting triangles, sew the short edge of the pink HST to the Diagram Q Unplugged blocks as shown. Make 4. These are sewn to the sides of the quilt.

For the corners, first sew the larger blue HST to the Diagram P Unplugged blocks. Note how half of the Unplugged blocks rotate.

Sew the short edge of the small blue HST to the pink corner squares.
Sew the pink corner unit to the Unplugged blocks as shown.
Make 4.

Note: Simplify the design by using a solid color for the corners.
Cut 2 18" squares, then cut once on the diagonal for the four corners.

Layout the quilt according to the diagram and sew in diagonal rows.

Quilt and finish as desired.

Ripples Coloring Page

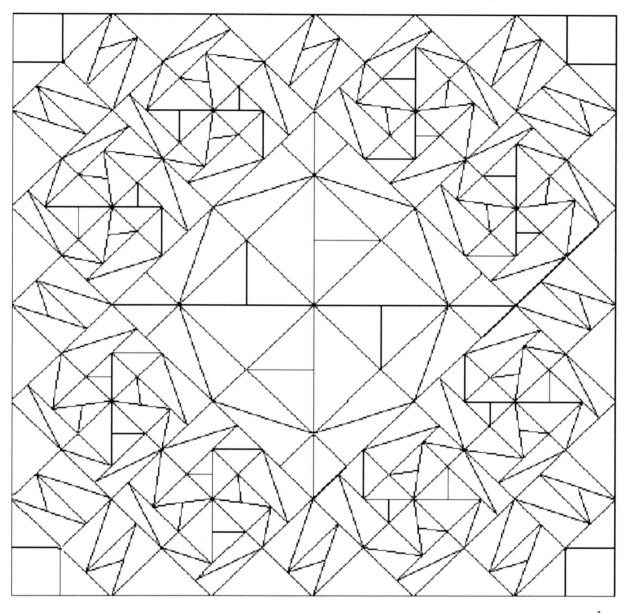

Tickle My Fancy

*Tickle My Fancy
sample created by
Barbara Harrell*

Tickle My Fancy
67-1/2" square
A, B & H templates

Fabric Requirements

1 - Yellow	3-2/3 yd	4 - Cream	2/3 yd
2 - Gold	½ yd	5 - Light Blue	1-1/4 yd
3 - Rust	2 yd	6 - Dark Blue	1-1/4 yd

Mosaic No 1(2)
12-1/2" blocks – Make 4

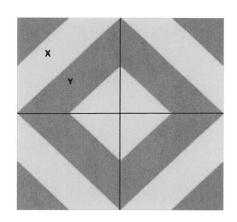

Diagram Piece, Color		# WOF Strips	Subcuts
X	Cream	6 at 2-3/4"	16 @ 9-1/2", 16 @ 5-1/2"
Y	Rust	6 at 2-3/4"	16 @ 9-1/2", 16 @ 5-1/2"

Sew the longer strips of X and Y together.
Press seams open.

Mark the center of both sides and the centers of the short X and Y strips.
Pin and sew alternate colors on each side.

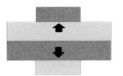

Use a 6-1/2" square ruler to cut units on-point. Line up the diagonal from the ruler with the middle seam and trim the excess triangles from each side.   Cut 16 units.

Sew 4 units to make a full block.
Make 4.

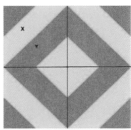

Star in a Knot Block
12-1/2", Make 9
A & B templates

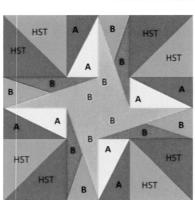

Diagram Piece, color		# WOF Strips	Template (# rectangles)	Subcuts
HST	Light Blue	3 at 4-7/8"	Squares at 4-7/8" (18)	36 HST
	Dark Blue	3 at 4-7/8"	Squares at 4-7/8" (18)	36 HST
A	Yellow	3 at 3-1/4"	A: 3-1/4" x 5" (18)	36 A left
	Dark Blue	3 at 3-1/4"	A: 3-1/4" x 5" (18)	36 A left
B	Rust	8 at 2"	*Not needed*	36 B side
	Light Blue	5 at 3-1/2"	*Not needed*	36 B base
	Gold	3 at 3-1/4"	B: 3-1/4" x 7" (18)	36 B right

Sew the light blue and dark blue HST into squares.
Make 36.

Sew the yellow and dark blue A triangles into rectangles.
Make 36.

Sew the pieced triangles by adding the orange B side triangles to the left side of the light blue base triangles.

Sew the gold B right-facing triangles to form rectangles.
Make 36.

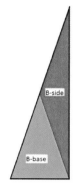
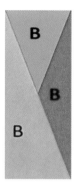

Sew the light blue side of the HST to the dark blue side of the A units. Make 36.

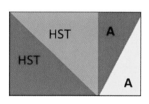

Sew the orange side of the B unit to the bottom make one quadrant.
Make 36.

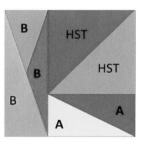

Rotate 4 quadrants to create the star.
Make 9.

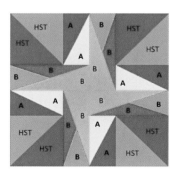

Left and Right Block
12-1/2" - Make 12
H template

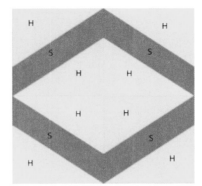

Diagram Piece, Color		# WOF Strips	Template (# rectangles)	Subcuts
H	Yellow	8 at 5-1/4"	H: 48 5-1/4" x 7"	48 H right, 48 H left
S	Rust	3 at 10"	Rectangles 2-1/4" x 10"	48 rectangles

To maximize a scrappy effect, you may need to use a design wall to layout the quarter sections before sewing the blocks. Be careful to keep the units in the proper orientation – the diamonds will not look right if units are rotated.

Sew 24 H right-facing triangles to the S rectangles. Place the long side of the triangle about 1-1/2 inches from the end of the middle strip.
Trim the units to 6-1/2".

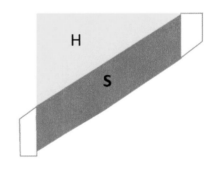

Add the remaining right-facing triangles to the opposite side, and square the unit to 6-1/2".

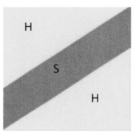

Repeat the process with the left-facing triangles: sew one triangle to the center strip, trim, then add the second triangle. Make 48 right-facing (uphill) units, and 48 left-facing (downhill) units.

Use two of each unit to form the final block. Make 12.

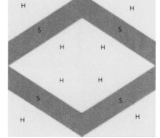

Layout the blocks on point, according to the diagram. Add corner and setting triangles before sewing into rows. Keeping the side and corner triangles the same color changes the look of the quilt, as shown in the photographs.

For the two-tone blue setting triangles: cut one 14" square of each color. Cut twice on the diagonal.

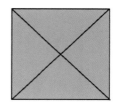

Pair two triangles together to form one setting triangle. Make 4.

For the yellow setting triangles, cut two 19" squares. Cut twice on the diagonal as above.

For the yellow corner triangles, cut two 11" squares. Cut *once* on the diagonal.

Note: the corner and setting triangles are OVERSIZED. Trim so that the sides are even, after the quilt top is assembled.

Tickle My Fancy Coloring Page

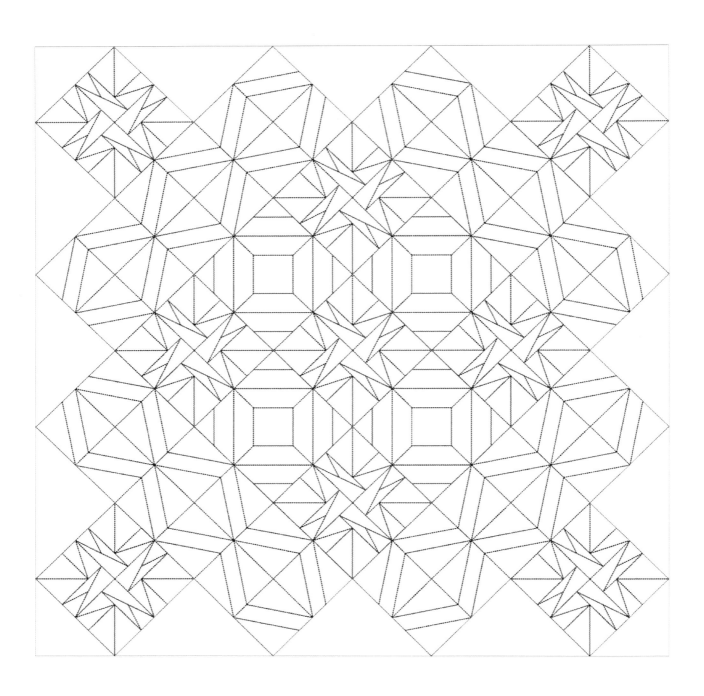

Echo

Echo
48" square or
54-1/2" sq with optional border
A, B, D, & H templates

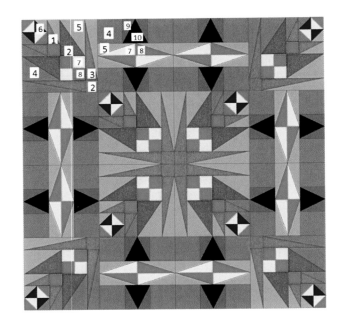

Fabric Requirements

1 - Pink 1	¼ yd	6 - Burgundy	1/8 yd
2 - Pink 2	7/8 yd	7 - Yellow	3/8 yd
3 - Pink 3	½ yd	8 - Green	½ yd
4 - Dark purple	1-1/4 yd + (3/8 yd optional border)	9 - Blue	1/3 yd + (½ yd optional border)
5 - Light purple	1- ½ yd	10 - Black	1/3 yd + (1/3 yd optional border)

Snapdragon
12" block
2 colorways - make 4 each
A, D, & H templates

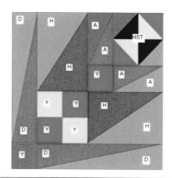

Diagram Piece, Color		# WOF Strips	Template (# rectangles)	Subcuts
HST	Dark purple	1 at 2-7/8"	Squares, 4 at 2-7/8"	8 HST
	Burgundy	1 at 2-7/8"	Squares, 8 at 2-7/8"	16 HST
	Light purple	1 at 2-7/8"	Squares, 4 at 2-7/8"	8 HST
	Yellow	1 at 2-7/8"	Squares, 8 at 2-7/8"	16 HST
	Green	1 at 2-7/8"	Squares, 8 at 2-7/8"	16 HST
Y	Green	2 at 2-1/2"	Squares, 24 at 2-1/2"	24 squares
	Yellow	1 at 2-1/2"	Squares, 16 at 2-1/2"	16 squares
	Pink 2	1 at 2-1/2"	Squares, 8 at 2-1/2"	8 squares
D	Dark purple	1 at 3-1/4"	D: 2 at 11"	4 D left
	Pink 3	4 at 3-1/4"	D: 8 at 11"	8 D left 8 D right
	Light purple	2 at 3-1/4"	D: 6 at 11"	12 D right
H	Dark purple	1 at 5-1/4"	H: 2 at 7"	4 H left
	Pink 2	2 at 5-1/4"	H: 8 at 7"	8 H right 8 H left
	Light purple	1 at 5-1/4"	H: 6 at 7"	12 H right
A	Dark purple	1 at 3-1/4"	A: 4 at 5"	8 A left
	Pink 1	1 at 3-1/4"	A: 8 at 5"	8 A right 8 A left
	Light purple	1 at 3-1/4"	A: 4 at 5"	8 right

Start with the 4-patch of half-square triangles.
Pair the triangles and sew as follows:
dark purple + burgundy – make 8; light purple + burgundy – make 8;
yellow + green – make 16

Assemble 8 units as shown in the diagram.

Sew the A rectangles together in 2 colorways.
Make 8 of each colorway:
left facing dark purple + pink 1, and right facing light purple + pink 1.

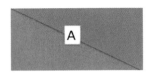

Using the HST unit from Step 1, the A rectangles, and 8
green Y squares, assemble the block as shown.

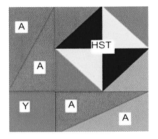

Sew 16 yellow and green Y squares into 8 4-patches.

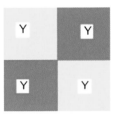

Sew the H rectangles together. Make the left version in 2 colorways:
4 with dark purple + pink 2, and another 4 with light purple + pink 2.

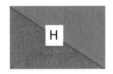
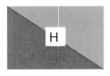

All the right facing H rectangles will be light purple + pink 2.

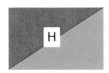

Attach the rectangles and the green + yellow 4-patch to the right-facing H
unit. Make 8.

Sew the left-facing H units to the HST unit. Make 4 with the light rectangles (version 1) and 4 with the dark rectangles (version 2).

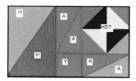
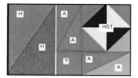

Add the four patch row to the bottom of the H unit rows. Make 4 of each colorway.

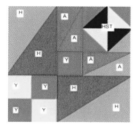
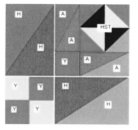

Sew the final round in the same manner as previous steps.
Sew the D rectangles together. Make the left version in 2 colorways, 4 with dark purple + pink 3, and another 4 with light purple + pink 3. All the right facing D rectangles will be light purple + pink 3.

Add the right-facing D rectangles to the pink 2 Y squares to make the bottom row of the block.

Add the left-facing D rectangles to the previous unit to complete the block in two versions. Make 4 of each colorway.

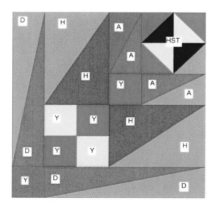
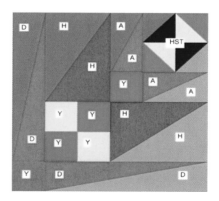

Lightning Bug
12" block, Make 8
A & B templates

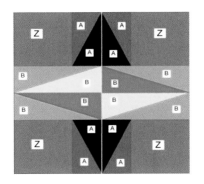

Diagram Piece, Color		# WOF Strips	Template (# rectangles)	Subcuts
Z	Dark purple	4 at 4-1/2"	Squares at 4-1/2" (32)	32 squares
A	Blue	2 @ 3-1/4"	A: 16 at 5"	16 A right 16 A left
	Black	2 @ 3-1/4"	A: 16 at 5"	16 A right 16 A left
B	Light purple	2 at 3-1/4"	B: 8 at 7"	16 B right
	Yellow	2 at 3-1/4"	B: 8 at 7"	16 B right
	Light Purple	2 at 3-1/4"	B: 8 at 7"	16 B left
	Green	2 at 3-1/4"	B: 8 at 7"	16 B left

Sew the A triangles together to form rectangles. 8 will face right, and 8 will face left.

Sew these rectangles together to form the middle square.

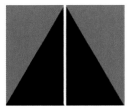

Sew this square between two dark purple Z squares to form rows. Make 16 rows.

Sew the B triangles into rectangles. Make 16 yellow and 16 green paired with the corresponding light purple triangles.

Sew these rectangles into larger two-color triangles.

Finish by sewing two units together to form a diamond unit. Make 8 diamond units.

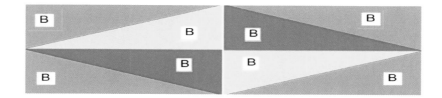

Complete the block by sewing the rows from step 1 onto the top and bottom of the diamond unit.
Make 8 blocks.

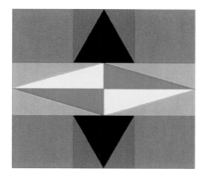

Lay out the blocks according to the diagram. The Snapdragon version 1 blocks form the center while the Snapdragon version 2 blocks are in the corners. The top and bottom Lightning Bug blocks are placed horizontally while the sides are placed vertically.

The photographs show a brown version of Echo with an additional outer border.

Use Template A-right to make 8 more triangle units from blue and black, matching those in the Lightning Bug block.

From blue, cut 8 squares at 4-1/2", and 4 rectangles at 4-1/2"x 8-1/2".

From dark purple, cut 8 rectangles at 4-1/2" x 12-1/2".

Make 4 rows as shown, with the black triangles in the center:

Attach 2 of these borders to the sides of the quilt.

Make 4 half-square triangles with Pink 2 and Green. Use 2 squares of each color, cut at 2-7/8 then cut once on the diagonal. Add a HST to each end of the remaining border units, and attach to the top and bottom of the quilt.

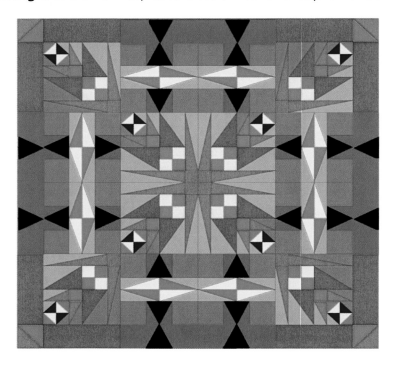

Quilt and finish as desired.

Echo Coloring Page

Spring Training

*Spring Training
sample created
by Shari Graves*

Spring Training
52-1/2" square
A, B, H, & K templates

Fabric Requirements

1- Grey	1-1/2 yd		4 – Tan	1-3/4 yd
2 - Black	¾ yd		5 – Red	1-1/4 yd
3 – White	5/8 yd			

On My Way
12-1/2" block – Make 4
B & K templates

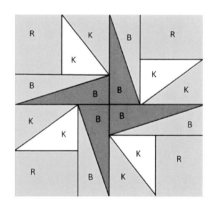

Diagram Piece, Color		# WOF Strips	Template (# rectangles)	Subcuts
R	Tan	2 at 3-1/2"	Rectangles 3-1/2" x 4-1/2" (16)	16 rectangles
K	Tan	1 at 3-1/2"	K1: 3-1/2" x 4" (8)	16 K1 right
	White	1 at 3-1/2"	K1: 3-1/2" x 4" (8)	16 K1 right
B	Tan	2 at 3-1/4"	B: 3-1/4" x 7" (8)	16 B right
	Grey	2 at 3-1/4"	B: 3-1/4" x 7" (8)	16 B right

Sew the K triangles together to form rectangles.
Make 16.

Attach an R unit to the white edge.
Make 16.

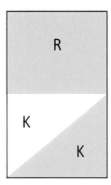

Sew the B triangles together to form rectangles.
Make 16.

Attach the B units to the left side of the R-K units to make
one quadrant of the On My Way Block.
Make 16.

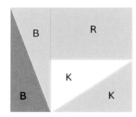

Rotate the quadrants to form a star and sew 4 quadrants together to make
the full block.
Make 4.

Prop Plane
12-1/2" block, Make 4
A & H templates

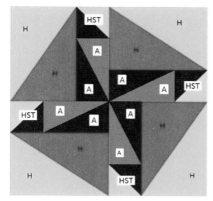

Diagram Piece, Color		# WOF Strips	Template (# rectangles)	Subcuts
HST	Tan	1 at 2-7/8"	Squares 2-7/8" (8)	16 HST
	Black	1 at 2-7/8"	Squares 2-7/8" (8)	16 HST
A	Grey	2 at 3-1/4"	A: 3-1/4" x 5" (8)	16 A right
	Black	2 at 3-1/4"	A: 3-1/4" x 5" (8)	16 A right
H	Tan	2 at 7"	H: 5-1/4" x 7" (8)	16 H left
	Red	2 at 7"	H: 5-1/4" x 7" (8)	16 H left

Pair the tan and black HST pieces together and sew 16 HST units. Trim to 2-1/2".

Sew the grey and black A triangles into rectangles. Make 16.

Sew the tan and red H triangles into rectangles. Make 16.

Sew the black side of the HST to the grey end of the A units as shown.
Make 16.

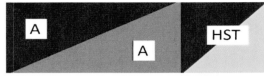

Sew the black edge to the red side of the H units to form one quadrant of the Prop Plane block.
Make 16.

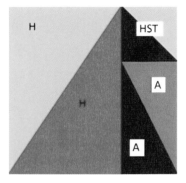

Rotate the quadrants to form a star and sew 4 quadrants together to make the full block.
Make 4.

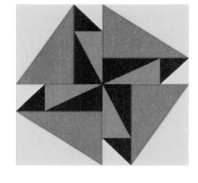

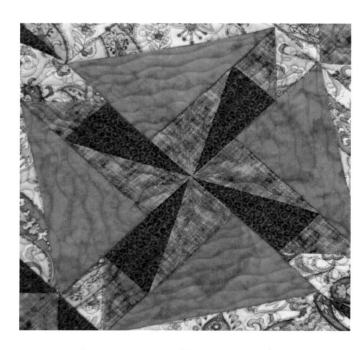

The Wreath block is made entirely from half square triangles. Note the color placement – one block has a solid center, and the other four have one side with a pop of color.

Wreath A – Make 1
(solid center)

Wreath B – Make 4
(colored side)

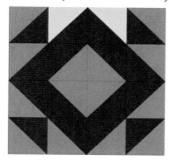

Cutting for Wreath Blocks

Diagram Color		# WOF Strips	Subcuts
HST	Black	4 at 3- 7/8"	40 squares to make 80 HST
	Grey	4 at 3- 7/8"	34 squares to make 68 HST
	Tan	1 at 3- 7/8"	6 squares to make 12 HST

Pair the black and tan triangles to make 12 HST units. Trim to 3-1/2".

Pair the grey and black triangles to make 68 HST units. Trim to 3-1/2".

Sew two of the grey HST as shown in step 1. Make 4 units for Wreath A.

Step 1:

Sew one tan HST to one grey HST as shown in step 2. Make 4 units for Wreath A.

Step 2:

Sew these units into one quadrant of the Wreath A block. Make 4.

Rotate so the tan fabrics are in the center, then sew the quadrants together to complete Wreath A.

Wreath B

Sew the 4 tan HST to a grey HST as shown in step 3. Make 4 facing the left, and 4 facing the right.

Step 3: Left   Right

Sew two grey HST along the black edge as shown in step 4. Make 8 with an uphill slant and 8 with a downhill slant.

Step 4: Uphill   Downhill

Sew these units together to form quadrants. Make 4 facing left and 4 facing right.

Sew two grey HST in pairs as shown in Step 5. Make 4 left and 4 right.
Step 5: Left   Right

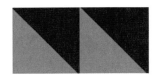

Sew the Step 5 units to the remaining uphill and downhill pairs to form the other half of the Wreath block. Make 8.

Sew the four quadrants together to create the Wreath B block. Make 4.

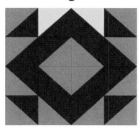

Assemble the rows with blocks on point. Refer to the diagram for block placement. Wreath A will be in the center, surrounded by Prop Plane and On My Way blocks, with Wreath B blocks in the corners.

Cutting for Setting Triangles

Diagram Color	# WOF Strips	Subcuts
White	1 at 8-5/8"	4 squares cut once to make 8 HST
Grey	5 at 1-1/2"	8 rectangles 1-1/2" x 10-1/2" 8 rectangles 1-1/2" x 13"
Red	5 at 3-1/4"	8 rectangles 3-1/4" x 11" 8 rectangles 3-1/4" x 13-1/2"

Assemble the setting triangles in the same fashion as a log cabin block.

Sew the short grey rectangle to one side of the white triangle

Add the long grey rectangle to the other side.

Add the short red rectangle to one side.

Add the long red rectangle to the other side.

Make 8 setting triangles. Attach to opposite ends of each row as shown in the diagram.
Sew rows together.

Cutting for Corner Triangles

Diagram Color	# WOF strips	Subcuts
Tan	1 at 13-1/2"	2 squares cut once to make 4 HST
Red	2 at 3-1/4"	4 rectangles 3-1/4" x 18"

Note: triangles will be oversized, then trimmed once quilt is assembled.

Sew the red strip along the base of the tan triangle. Make 4.

Attach to corners of quilt to complete the quilt top then trim so the quilt top is square.

Quilt and finish as desired.

Spring Training Coloring Page

Free Motion Quilting Ideas

Finding the perfect motif for a quilt can be a challenge. The AnglePlay® blocks are based on triangles, so here are some ideas to fill those spaces, using the seam lines as boundaries:

It can be effective to ignore the piecing lines and fill the entire block with an entire design. The spiral rose gives a softer look or use the polygon spiral for a bold graphic feel.

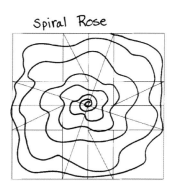

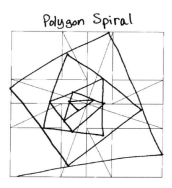

I like to quilt with freeform feathers, and I can usually make them fit into any area of a quilt.

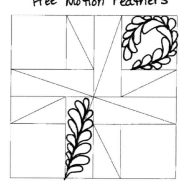

Find more quilting ideas at TrueBlueQuilts.com. Free Motion Mondays are dedicated to sharing a variety of quilting designs.

About the Authors

Mary McElvain

At Mary's first quilt guild meeting, a friend leaned over to her and whispered, "Some of these people quilt every day!" At the time such an idea seemed preposterous. Now, Mary is one of those people. She spends time in her quilt studio working on a variety of projects. Mary made her first quilt in the 1970's and then took a hiatus while working as a psychiatric mental health nurse. She returned to full time quilting in 2003, opening a quilt shop in Avondale, AZ called Cotton Fields Quilt & Knit. Since the shop closed at the end of 2008, Mary now has the luxury of quilting with friends, teaching at a local shop and designing quilts and writing patterns with her daughter. Mary encourages all quilters to feed their creative passions and continue to explore new dimensions in this fabulous artistic craft.

Andi Stanfield

The quilting addiction took hold soon after Andi started working in her mother's quilt shop. Two years after making her first quilt top, she purchased a longarm and started designing patterns as bonus class materials for Cotton Fields Quilt & Knit. Nowadays, she fits quilting into vacations from her day job as a high school teacher. You might even find her sewing in a hotel room while at her daughter's figure skating competitions! Keep up with her latest projects at TrueBlueQuilts.com.

Made in the USA
Columbia, SC
03 December 2022

72659016R00062